# SINGAPORE

Photography by Ian Lloyd
Text by Ilsa Sharp

**HARRAP COLUMBUS**

Published by Harrap Limited
19-23 Ludgate Hill, London EC4M 7PD
and The Guidebook Company Limited,
The Penthouse, 20 Hollywood Road,
Central, Hong Kong

Title spread
*Sunset over the 'city-scape' of
Singapore's central business
district, Southeast Asia's Wall
Street. This is the view from
the southwest of Singapore
island, at the Straits of
Singapore that border the South
China Sea. Just over 60,000
vessels use the port every year,
making it one of the world's
busiest harbours.*

Right
*The Singaporean typically
reaches for the sky. Excellence,
efficiency, service, quality, and
cleanliness are among the
virtues he values. The
Republic's dynamic national
airline, Singapore Airlines,
epitomizes these virtues: here
the airline's yellow-on-navy,
blue bird-motif is carefully
spruced up to match its image.*

Pages 6-7
*The port of Singapore never
sleeps, clearing more than 500
shipping lines a year, 24 hours
a day. Middleman to the
world's trade with Southeast
Asia, Singapore handles about
50 million freight tonnes of
cargo a year, 32 million of
them containerized, through
ultra-modern facilities like this
container terminal.*

Pages 8-9
*Recently Singapore has begun
to refurbish architectural
masterpieces like these. This
'Chinese neo-classical'
architecture, so elegantly
tailored to the tropical climate,
is unique to Singapore and a
few Malaysian towns. As a
style it was at its peak in the
early 20th century.*

Pages 10-11
*Highly disciplined when it
comes to mass collective
action, loyal Singaporeans line
up perfectly in place at a
National Day rally to form a
human tableau depicting the
red-and-white national flag,
with its crescent moon and five
stars. Singapore's National Day
on 9 August is famed for such
pageantry.*

Text and captions by Ilsa Sharp

Photography by Ian Lloyd

Designed by Joan Law Design & Photography
Colour separations by Rainbow Graphic Arts Co., Ltd.
Jacket colour separations by Sakai Lithocolour
Printed in Hong Kong

ISBN: 0-7471-0115-9

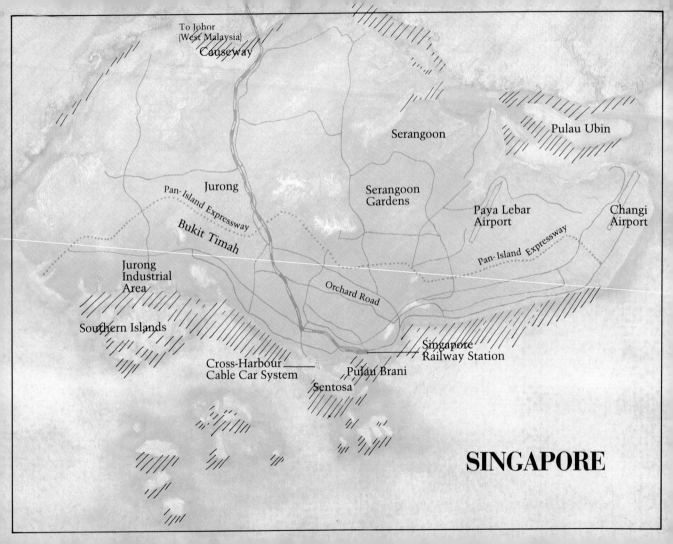

# INTRODUCTION

'INSTANT ASIA' was once Singapore's own crude tag for itself. The implication was that the island republic, positioned at a world transportation crossroads, with neighbouring peninsular Malaysia to the north, eastern Malaysia (Borneo) to the east and Indonesia to the south, had almost all the attractions of the Southeast Asian region and that one need not travel further to find them.

Certainly Singapore boasts a multi-ethnic blend of the region's peoples which is even more various than the bland official statistics of 76.3 percent Chinese, 15 percent Malay, 6.4 percent Indian and 2.3 percent 'Other'.

The mosques, temples, churches, synagogues and shrines of Singapore cater to an array of faiths, including Islam, Buddhism, Christianity, Hinduism, Sikhism, Judaism and Zoroastrianism.

To appreciate the essence of this cultural jumble with its bright, shiny Western hi-tech exterior (visible from the moment you arrive in the dazzling chrome and super-efficiency of modern Changi Airport) and yet quintessentially Asian interior, you really need longer than the average visitor's 3.5-day stay.

This 622-square-kilometre (240-square-mile) island republic has passed through the industrial revolution to post-industrial society, all within the quarter of a century or so since independence in 1959 from the British. They themselves gained sovereignty over the island in 1824, five years after Sir Stamford Raffles had established a trading post there for the British East India Company, but this was certainly not Singapore's beginning. The island, strategically situated at the western entrance to the South China Sea, has been the lynchpin in the ambitions of both the Indian and Chinese civilizations. According to Malay mythology, Singapore was founded by a prince. Having been washed ashore on the island he saw an animal he took to be a lion and, believing this to be auspicious, founded Singapura, the Lion City.

Singapore's political system is a British-style parliamentary democracy. The government is overwhelmingly dominated by the People's Action Party, which has been in power since 1959, led by the towering figure of Prime Minister Lee Kuan Yew, architect of the nation. Never afraid of controversy, Lee has instituted government-sponsored matchmaking for the country's well-educated in the belief that graduates breed graduates.

The result of this paternalistic government has been a highly disciplined, largely obedient people whose considerable natural energies are engaged more in the pursuit of wealth than in the arenas of politics, philosophy or the arts.

Lee has signed an effective social contract with the majority of his people by keeping their rice bowls overflowing with the good things of life. Singapore is all that it boasts — safe, clean, green.

A determined push for industrialisation began in the late 1960s, partly as a result of the withdrawal from the Malaysian federation in 1965 and partly due to the economic shock waves resulting from the British troop withdrawal in 1968.

The combination of a natural national gift for commerce and a strategic geographic position at the hub of a booming region rapidly brought Singapore heady economic success.

This success made possible enormous government housing programmes, to resettle Singaporeans from their traditional villages or *kampungs* into smart high-rise estates. These now accommodate 85 percent of the population. Yet this affluence and technological know-how have not completely erased remnant traditions.

The Singaporean Chinese businessman, sweeping out of his automated factory in a sleek limousine, might well be bound for a Taoist temple to consult the *feng shui* geomancer on where to build his new home. A suitably propitious location is as important to his success as economic efficiency.

*The typically Straits Chinese blend of East and West can be seen in the windows and roofs of many gracious pre-war buildings. Straits Chinese (locally-born Chinese) trace their ancestry back to 15th-century Malacca in Malaysia.*

*Other buildings betray other strands in the tapestry that is Singapore — these slightly Arabic yet still colonial windows, for example.*

Similarly, the Indian cashier at Komala Vilas, an old-favourite, vegetarian restaurant, still wears his traditional white *lungi* (wraparound skirt), hangs multi-limbed Hindu images and idols all around his shop, and eats with his fingers from a banana-leaf plate. Yet he uses an electronic calculator to tot up your bill and his closed-circuit television helps him keep an eye on tables upstairs.

To add to the convenient confluence of Western comforts with the exotica of the East and the competing pulls of tradition and modernity are little gems of colonial history. The gracious 19th-century Raffles Hotel, a bastion of the British Empire, now lies in the shadow of the 73-storey Westin Hotel, that itself is part of a three-quarters-of-a-billion US dollar complex, yet this has not ruined the very special flavour of a Singapore Gin Sling sipped at sunset in the hotel's gracious Palm Court.

For the traveller, the chaos of cultural confusion that Singapore presents is a boon. It means Western comforts such as hot showers, bidets and US prime-rib, side by side with the exotica of the East.

Singapore is 'visitor-friendly'. Its people won independence from the British virtually without any blood being shed, they have kept the British street-names and lovingly maintained the 19th-century statue of their British founder Sir Stamford Raffles, set in the elegant colonial compound of Empress Place. Today the visitors are mostly tourists, but Singaporeans genuinely like foreigners, and they need to, for there are currently more than three million tourists swelling their own population of 2.5 million every year. Four million are expected by 1990.

This phenomenon was gloomily foreseen by British snob J.S.M. Rennie, who snorted in the 1930s: 'One is forced to opine that Singapore's main business will become that of a health resort and place of visit for American and Australian trippers.'

And so Singaporeans are kindly indulgent to the foreigner, rarely pointing out his blunders of etiquette. The visitor needs to learn from the row of shoes outside a Singaporean home that one should enter barefoot, and that the wet floor and bucket of water in a Singaporean bathroom indicate that most Singaporeans wash after relieving themselves.

There is no language problem for the visitor, however. The multi-lingual Singaporean speaks at a minimum his mother tongue, English, Malay, and often a couple more Chinese dialects too. Even his English can be spoken on two levels — formal and informal. The formal is for you, but keep your ears pricked to overhear Singaporeans talking informally to one another and you will find a kind of English almost incomprehensible to the outsider. It is a language that results from the combination of the dominant English language with Asian mother tongues. Jestingly referred to as 'Singlish' by locals, it is a vibrant street language, officially discouraged but flourishing nonetheless. The most typical example (and probably your lasting memory of Singlish) is the word *la* (also spelt *lah*), a Malay suffix used by Singaporeans of all races to emphasize a point or just to round off a sentence, *la*!

Once upon a time a pirates' lair and even not so long ago 'Sin City of the East' (as immortalized in Paul Theroux's '60s novel, *Saint Jack*) Singapore has mellowed. The secret triad societies were rubbed out long ago and the last tiger — a circus escapee — was shot in 1902 under Raffles' billiards room, so the legend goes.

Not that the glamour has gone. The new arrival still feels much as Joseph Conrad did in the 1880s, coming into Singapore harbour: 'I saw brown, bronze, yellow faces, the black eyes, the glitter, the colour of an Eastern crowd.' And you may still look from your hotel window, as Jim in Conrad's *Lord Jim* did, 'over the thickets of gardens, beyond the roofs of the town, over the fronds of palms growing on the shore, at that roadstead which is the thoroughfare to the East — at the roadstead dotted by garlanded islets, lighted by festal sunshine, its ships like toys...'

This is still one of the busiest ports in the world, an international rendezvous for the very same adventurers and dreamers that people Conrad's stories, living 'in a crazy maze of plans, hopes, dangers, enterprises, ahead of civilization, in the dark places of the sea.' A global city.

This is a place too where southern-Indian Hindu Singaporeans, mostly Tamils, take to the streets every year between January and February with a cartwheel of spears piercing their body in the festival of *Thaipusam*, a demonstration of piety for their gods.

It is also a place where you might turn a corner at the back of a skyscraper and walk straight into a classical Chinese street-opera. The makeshift stage is peopled with willowy maidens clad in Ming-Dynasty robes, and bearded warriors, their shoulders strangely adorned with waving flags, their faces grotesquely made up in black, white, blue and red. Together they wail in seeming harmony with the clash of cymbals and gongs.

*Sir Stamford Raffles, who first claimed Singapore as a trading post for the British East India Company, is revered by Singaporeans.*

If you relish the bizarre there is Tiger Balm Gardens, with its grotesque grottoes and gruesome murals. Singapore soon will inject more than US$20 million to transform this one-time Chinese millionaire's playground into a 7.7-hectare pleasure park. The narrow back alleys of Chinatown are still there, although they have become safely sanitized hunting grounds for the shutter-bug. They still offer a fascinating store-house of oddities such as Chinese funeral goods. These are paper models of all the trappings of the affluent life from cars to televisions and computers, which are burnt at a person's death to ensure well-being in the afterlife.

The Singapore passion for food also endures. The old-style food-stalls still exist, but now in superbly clean new centres, both indoor and outdoor. Airconditioning makes the indoor restaurant more comfortable, no less 'authentic' than the outdoor one. Both still offer the same mouthwatering dishes — fragrant chicken-rice, oyster omelette, fried noodles, carrot-cake, Indian breads, Malay *rojak* salad and shashlik-like satay.

*The Merlion statue — a recently-created symbol for Singapore, the 'Lion City'.*

The favourite locations for this local 'hawker food' are Newton Circus, Cuppage Road Market, the Satay Club at the Esplanade, and a host of new food centres in prime Orchard Road complexes. Old stalwarts like the Rendezvous and Fatty's have moved into smarter premises but retain the style of old.

Seafood restaurants dishing out the famed chilli crab, garlic mussels (*tua tow*), steamed prawns and other shelled delights often are far from the sea nowadays — Palm Beach at the National Stadium, Long Beach at Bedok Road, Seafood Palace at Pasir Panjang and myriad others.

New additions are classy but still good value for money, from upmarket Li Bai's *nouvelle Cantonnaise* cuisine at the Sheraton Towers Hotel, the charming chic of Prego's Italian restaurant in Raffles City and one of the best Western salad buffets in town at Pete's Place in the Hyatt Hotel.

New lifestyles have brought Western-style health-food corners like Steeple's Deli in the Tanglin Shopping Centre and Checkers at Orchard Point, but also a plethora of fast-food hamburger joints, swarming with young Singaporeans who seem mysteriously to prefer such imports to their own delicious fare. Fiery southern-Indian meat and fish curries are found around Racecourse Road in 'Little India', while the more spiritual, cooling qualities of first-class Indian vegetarian food, northern and southern, are served graciously in elegant surroundings by a religious cooperative at Annalakshmi (no alcohol and no cigarettes here), in the Excelsior Hotel arcade.

*The Supreme Court dome — legacy of colonial architecture of the 1930s.*

For those who can bear to give up the pleasures of the flesh, there are few meals more pleasing than a crisp Buddhist vegetarian one — at the Happy Realm in Pearl Centre, the Kwan Inn in Victoria Street, the Fut Sai Gai in Kitchener Road or the Loke Woh Yuen in Tanjong Pagar.

*A Malay cultural dancer relives the vanished rural lifestyle of her forbears. Malays comprise 15 percent of Singapore's population.*

*Mother and baby watch the world go by — windows and doors are ever ajar in Singapore's humid heat.*

*Indians represent just over six percent of Singaporeans; most of them are dark-skinned Tamils of southern-Indian origin.*

The Hainanese-Chinese waiters of colonial renown still staff the elite Tanglin Club and the Cricket Club as well as colonial hotels such as Raffles or the Goodwood Park (the latter with its Teutonic turret also claims 19th-century fame as the German Club).

Singapore not only has retained the traditional forms of its multi-cultural heritage but also has developed its own indigenous culture. The Straits Chinese provide perhaps the most developed example. They are Malayanized Chinese, who are descendants from the old Chinese families of 16th-century Malacca in neighbouring Malaysia, but who now are Chinese only in name. In Singapore the Straits Chinese have become distinctive for the *Peranakan* culture of the *babas* (male) and the *nonyas* (female).

There is an elegant official preservation project at Peranakan Place and Emerald Hill Road, just off the Orchard Road tourist belt, dedicated to these urbane, sophisticated people, and also to their coconut milk and chilli-laced cuisine.

Recently Singapore has shown much greater respect for its own heritage. There are plans to preserve the old colonial area around the cricket pitch or *padang* (as an area of museums and cultural centres), the 'Little India' of Serangoon Road, Chinatown itself, around the Singapore River, and *Kampong Glam*, the centre of Islamic Singapore.

The *Kampong Glam* is not always on standard tour itineraries, but is well worth a visit. In a humble alley called Sultan Gate (just up Beach Road from Raffles and past Arab Street) amid minareted mosques, Arab textile traders and Islamic calligraphers still cluster around the decaying palace of the one-time Sultan of Singapore, who leased his island to the British in 1819. Some of the residents in this area still use the Malay title of *Tengku* (Prince).

In the old colonial area the cricket pitch is flanked by the domed Supreme Court and City Hall. On these imposing steps in 1945 Lord Louis Mountbatten, British Supreme Allied Commander in Southeast Asia, took the surrender of the Japanese forces which had occupied Singapore in 1942. This did not, however, salvage British prestige in the eyes of Singaporeans who had seen their former masters humiliated by the Japanese.

The iconoclastic Japanese occupation together with the communist-inspired and racial riots of the turbulent 1950s and 1960s rank as the most historical formative experiences of the Singaporean nation.

Looming above the cricket pitch stands Fort Canning Hill. This was once the preserve of the Malay kings of the 14th century. Along Serangoon Road's 'Little India' pause to breathe in the aromatic perfumes of jasmine and spices, welter in the riotous colour of silk and brocade saris and the haunting drums and chanting of ornately decorated Indian temples, and have your fortune read by a brightly-coloured parrot that selects from cards on the pavement. Then head out of town.

Northward-bound along the Bukit Timah Expressway you will find Singapore's marvellous Zoological Gardens at Mandai, an 'open zoo' with no bars. On your right and left are the last remnants of the 130-million-year-old tropical rainforest that once covered all Singapore.

The 75-hectare Bukit Timah Nature Reserve, which (little known even to Singaporeans) nestles in the centre of the island, complete with wild monkeys, flying lemurs, pythons, cobras and scorpions, is now a manageable forest, well-trailed and hard to get lost in. In 1855 man-eating tigers here almost provoked a serious emergency.

Towards the west is industrial Jurong, where the factories are skilfully camouflaged behind the greenery of the Chinese and Japanese Gardens. Here you can also see the Jurong Bird Park and its stunning, walk-in aviary, the largest in the world.

Island-hopping around Singapore's 57 offshore islands provides another escape route from the bustling city. Particularly attractive are undeveloped Pulau Ubin to the north and St Johns or Kusu to the south.

Sentosa Island, also off the south coast, sandwiched between Indonesia and mainland Singapore's Mount Faber, boasts a world-class wax museum, including a rivetting display on the trials of Japanese for war crimes held after World War II. Sentosa, which is underrated by jet-setting Singaporeans, also offers gentle country walks, specialized museums — the Coralarium, the Rare Stone Museum, the Maritime Museum, the Butterfly Park and soon an 'Underwater World' extravaganza — and some excellent, safe swimming off beautiful beaches.

If you go to the island on a weekend, the hordes of raucous youngsters shoulder-toting huge 'ghetto-blaster' cassette-players will remind you that Singapore is above all a young country. Like the young everywhere, it swaggers somewhat, but never-theless has a vulnerable heart.

*More than 76 percent of Singaporeans are Chinese, most of them descendants of southern-Chinese immigrants. It is the Chinese who set the nation's cultural tone.*

Cool pastels and shady arcades
distinguish one of Singapore's
preservation projects,
Peranakan Place, in Emerald
Hill off Orchard Road. It is
named after the locally-born
and Malayanized Peranakans or
Straits Chinese, masters of this
style.

Old and new jostle for
attention in Singapore's city
centre. The 19th-century
Cricket Club presides over the
cricket green. The white clock-
tower of the 1902 Victoria
Memorial Hall is behind it, and
the domed Supreme Court of
the 1930s is to the right.
Beyond Singapore River and
the skyscrapers of the financial
district to the southwest, lie
the cloud-swathed hills of
Indonesia.

An unusual side view from Bras Basah
Road of Raffles, one of the world's great
hotels, that dates back to 1887. Now
slated for restoration, Raffles was founded
by an Armenian family named Sarkies
and has become part of the folklore of the
British Empire.

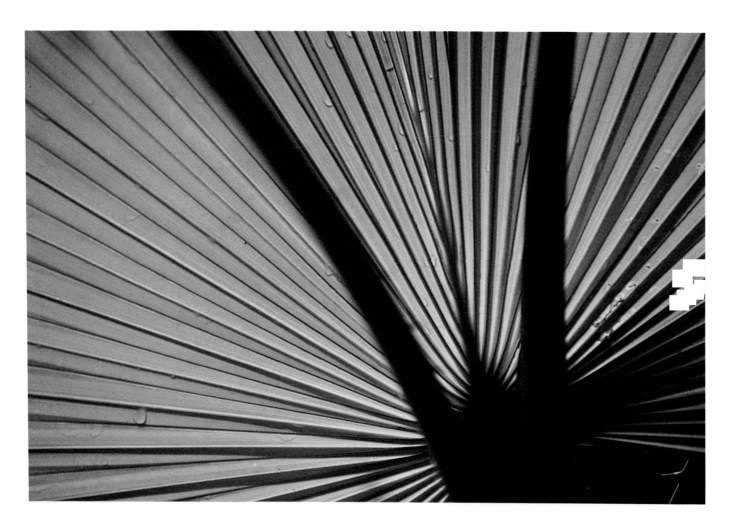

Tall Travellers' Palms are synonymous with Raffles and its open-air Palm Court, where daily hundreds of Singapore Slings are served to admiring visitors. The famous gin sling cocktail was invented at Raffles' bar in 1915.

'Raffles stands for all the fables of the exotic East', remarked British novelist Somerset Maugham, a regular guest during the 1920s and 30s. Maugham wrote several of his stories at the hotel.

Constructed in 1887, Queen Victoria's Jubilee year, the National Museum building with its gleaming dome came to symbolize the museum's role as a centre of Western scholarship in the region. Today the building is also home to the National Museum Art Gallery with its permanent collection of more than 600 works.

The National Museum's rotunda lobby is covered by a soaring 90-foot-tall (27.4-metre) dome. A treasure-house of Southeast Asian artefacts (it includes a 3,000-piece jade collection), the museum is a fitting tribute to its namesake Sir Stamford Raffles, himself a man of science and an avid collector.

The Tan Kim Seng fountain sits in the National Museum grounds. In 1857 Tan donated S$13,000 to the colonial government of Singapore for the construction of a fresh water supply. The donation was disregarded by the authorities and only in 1882, prompted by a guilty conscience, did they erect this fountain in his memory.

The Singapore river has served as a major artery for trade and commerce. Old Chinese sampans and bumboats once wound their way along the river with the help of the eyes painted on their bows. Today the river is bordered by the gleaming skyscrapers of 20th-century Singapore.

Tropical nights are inviting after the hot noonday sun, and Singaporeans instinctively take to the streets for their evening meal, dining under the stars amid a festival of light and colour and a babel of sound. Street-side hawkers' stalls have traditionally offered the best, most authentic and cheapest food.

At the very centre of
Singapore's premier shopping
and tourist district lies the
Orchard Road-Scotts Road
junction. For decades, C.K.
Tang's pagoda-style department
store has been a landmark
building for shoppers — the
store, with its high-rise sister
venture, Dynasty Hotel, still
sits at this corner.

Singaporeans work hard, but
they know how to play hard
too. National Day, May Day
and Chinese New Year are
among the many festivals that
give Singaporeans an excuse to
get out on the streets in their
fancy-dress best.

*The many smiling faces of Singapore: (clockwise) Chinese youth — in Singapore far from inscrutable; the Malay — ever gracious and sunny-tempered; the classical Indian beauty — colourful as a rainbow in her traditional sari.*

*The older generation still remembers a very different Singapore, whether under the British colonials up to 1959 or under the Japanese occupation from 1942-45, when Chinese resistance fighters waged a valiant guerrilla war with the invaders.*

Emerald Hill, painstakingly conserved, is a 'museum' of the elegant lifestyle of the Straits Chinese in the 1920s and 30s. The locally-born Straits Chinese were culturally fully Malayanized, and they were also social reformers and admirers of the West.

A Malay House, Singapore

As late as the 1920s, large tracts of Singapore were little more than swampland and tidal mangrove forest.

*Malay fishing villages built on stilts at the water's edge were still a common sight up to the mid-1960s.*

The architectural style which flowered in Singapore and in Malaysia's Penang and Malacca at the turn of the century is known as Chinese-Baroque for its fusion of neo-classical European styles with elaborate oriental ornamentation.

Typical of the style is the swinging saloon-door or pintu pagar entrance (top left) with its fine gold-leaf decoration, the ceramic wall-tiles on the lower half of the wall, and the barred, shuttered windows without glass for maximum circulation of air.

Old ways persist. The burning of joss or incense sticks keeps evil spirits away from the home. Here the housewife reveres the spirits of her ancestors in a prayer typical of local occultist-Taoist beliefs.

About 85 percent of Singaporeans now live in high-rise public housing estates provided by the government in a massive resettlement programme that began in the 1960s. Recently-built apartments are roomy and luxurious and most estates are now equipped with a wide range of amenities, including shops, schools, swimming pools and jogging tracks.

Approximately eight percent of Singapore's population is over 60 years old. True to Asian tradition, the government actively encourages family unity and rewards sons and daughters who keep their parents in comfort at home.

Coconut plantations in the northern and far western reaches of Singapore island, and on the many offshore islands, recall a rural past. More than half the island is built up now, and only six percent of it is farmed.

Fish farms abound in the more rural areas. With almost 40 fish farms, Singapore is a major exporter of aquarium fish, chiefly to Europe and the United States. The island exports more than S$47 million of aquarium fish and over S$4 million of aquatic plants a year.

Following page
The kelong, or traditional fish-trap, is a common and dramatic sight, silhouetted against the twilight skies of the seas off the northern coast of Singapore. At night lights are used to attract the fish into a huge fishing net which is suspended beneath the water in the area fenced off by the kelong poles.

Childhood is particularly golden on a tropical island like Singapore, where youngsters can cavort almost naked in the sun and then cool off in sparkling waters. More than a third of Singaporeans are under 21 years old.

Village, or kampung life, especially typical among the Malays, persists in idyllic pockets like this. Malays who are also Muslims, live simple, traditional lives; they are very house-proud and also devout gardeners. Although they dislike dogs — as these are proscribed in the Koran — they love cats.

Following page
Traditional fishing boats

Singapore boasts as many as 350 orchid farms. These gorgeous tropical flowers are native to Singapore and bloom in profusion here. With exports worth S$10.34 million annually, this is big business. Intensive research and careful breeding have produced many completely new hybrids.

Bamboo groves reminiscent of classical Chinese paintings are one of the glories of the parks and gardens in Singapore.

As the blazing sun declines in the late afternoon, the petals of the lotus unfold on the ponds and lakes of Singapore's gardens. The lotus symbolizes purity and is valued by the Chinese both as a medicine and as a food.

Jurong, on the western side of the island, prides itself on being more than a mere industrial estate. This Chinese garden, modelled on a 1,000-year-old Sung-Dynasty garden, is like an oasis among the factories.

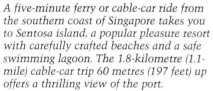

A five-minute ferry or cable-car ride from the southern coast of Singapore takes you to Sentosa island, a popular pleasure resort with carefully crafted beaches and a safe swimming lagoon. The 1.8-kilometre (1.1-mile) cable-car trip 60 metres (197 feet) up offers a thrilling view of the port.

Top right
A wax effigy of Lieutenant General Arthur Percival, the British army commander who surrendered Singapore to the Japanese in 1942 (in khaki, standing on the right), supervises the defeated Japanese as they in turn sign their surrender document in 1945. This is one of the many fascinating recreations of history to be seen at Sentosa's wax museum.

Bottom right
Sentosa's Musical Fountain: every night countless, luridly-lit water sprays leap and dance in rhythm to the tempo of lively music.

*The call to the Muslim faithful echoes daily from the minarets of the gold-domed Sultan Mosque (1924) through the streets of old* Kampong Glam, *Singapore's Arab-Malay quarter. This quarter was once the royal preserve of the Sultan of Singapore.*

*Fort Canning Hill was once the Forbidden Hill of the Malay kings of Temasek, as ancient Singapore was then known. The remains of a British cemetery of the mid-19th century add to the aura of mysterious and at times ghostly peace that envelopes the graciously landscaped hill today.*

*The century-old streets and shophouses of Chinatown offer new surprises and delights at every corner, and not least of these is the architecture itself.*

*Singapore is the emporium of Southeast Asia and basketware fashioned from rattan, the springy, native cane, floods in from neighbouring countries to fill the island's bazaars.*

*In Chinatown garish Chinese calligraphy advertises merchants' wares and services from the shaded sidewalks. Older people live life much as they always have, bargaining over street-market fruit, or spending the hot afternoons away at the roadside watching passersby.*

*Chinatown, to the southwest of Singapore River, was set aside for the Chinese by Sir Stamford Raffles in his town plan of 1822.*

This mobile peddler hawks his painted masks, some funny, others grotesque or downright scary, from a wheeled card hitched to a bicycle. While some may depict traditional Chinese folk heroes, or opera roles, others represent Western cartoon characters such as Mickey Mouse.

A Peranakan or Straits Chinese wedding is a rare sight today. Here the nonya or Peranakan woman dons bridal finery for an elaborate ceremony traditionally lasting 12 days.

Following page
As local fruits come into season, Singaporeans take to the streets for an orgy of fruit-buying, pinching and sampling the goods shamelessly, haggling the prices ruthlessly. Among their favourites are the duku and langsat seen here.

**Left**

*As well as finding tropical fruits native to Asia, you can get almost any kind of fruit from anywhere in the world at Singapore's fruit markets, including apples and oranges from the West, lychees and longans from China.*

**Above**

*You could write a whole book just about the prickly, stinking, sensuously-fleshed durian, the king of all Southeast Asian fruit. The durian is a Singaporean obsession, almost mystical in nature. Foreigners usually find the fruit and its odour a little harder to appreciate than local people do.*

**Bottom four**

*Singaporeans call these* kueh *(pronounced kway), using the Malay word for cake or biscuit.* Kueh *are nearly all brightly coloured, ranging from sticky red-for-prosperity Chinese ones filled with thick brown sugar or mashed sweet beans, to flaky sweet biscuits, to the truly Malay or Straits Chinese coconut slices and layered* agar-agar *(seaweed) jellies.*

Singapore's carnival is the annual Chingay
Procession, a traditional Chinese
celebration of spring, that is now usually
staged the first weekend after Chinese
New Year. A multi-racial synthesis of East
and West, Chingay today incorporates
everything from Chinese stilt-walkers and
Malay and Indian horse-dancers (kuda
kepang), to elements of Hollywood and
Disneyland.

*Lunar New Year is the biggest festival in a crowded festive calendar and just about the only time the Chinese stop working. After a few days' peace and quiet during family reunions at home, the city erupts into a clashing of gongs and cymbals, a riot of lion and dragon dances, and the streets and squares are crammed with spectators and revellers.*

*Thaipusam is an awe-inspiring ritual. Devotees of the Hindu god Lord Subramaniam, son of Lord Siva, pierce their flesh with an elaborate cartwheel of interconnected spears and lances (the* kavadi*) in thanks for prayers answered.*

*Thus burdened, they sing and march the several miles from Perumal Temple in Serangoon Road to the Thandayuthapani Temple on Tank Road, home of the horse-drawn chariot of Lord Subramaniam. Very few of them show pain or even bleed. Singapore is one of the few places left in which to view this exotic ritual, for it has largely died out in its homeland, southern India.*

During the festival of Hari Raya Puasa at the end of the fasting month known as Ramadan, the mosques of Singapore are filled with the Muslim faithful. Muslims represent 16 percent of Singapore's 2.5 million total population.

Men and women worship separately. The men dress in wrap-around sarong-skirts and wear either the black songkok hat or the white skull cap, indicating that they have made the long pilgrimage to Mecca. This qualifies them for the title of Haji.

Doors, walls, ceilings and altars in Singapore's Chinese temples are richly adorned with a confusing pantheon of spirits, scholars, warriors, saints, gods and demons. This is typical of the multi-faceted nature of Buddhism.

Here the two traditional door gods guard the temple gates (left) and a paper effigy (above) of the Devil King goes up in flames at the Festival of the Hungry Ghosts. This falls on the Seventh Moon, when neglected and potentially evil ghosts wander freely in the human world.

Insect and animal symbols, as varied as butterflies and bats (the latter are believed to bring good luck), are important in Chinese religion and are frequently woven into temple hangings.

The dragon is one of the 12 creature symbols on the Chinese lunar calendar. In Chinese mythology, the dragon is a divine, auspicious and benevolent creature, in contrast to its role in Western legend. The year 1988 was the most recent Year of the Dragon.

Tiger Balm Gardens is the creation of the Aw brothers, more widely known as the manufacturers of the famous, cure-all Tiger Balm ointment, which made them millionaires. The Gardens feature scenes of morality and immorality, of Heaven and Hell; the effect is rather like a prolonged sermon in cartoons.

Few zoos in the world could offer you
breakfast with an orang-utan, but
Singapore's Zoological Gardens does.
Here's a local star, the shaggy matron Ah
Meng, with a Singaporean admirer. The
Singapore zoo, set in 90 hectares of
luxuriant natural jungle, boasts the
world's largest social colony of the rare
and endangered orang-utan ape from
Sumatra and Borneo.

Colourful American macaw parrots greet
the visitor to the Jurong Bird Park, another
garden attraction nestled in the Jurong
industrial estate. The 20-hectare bird park
houses 3,500 birds of 400 species and the
world's largest walk-in aviary.

*Chinese opera is as refined an art as Western opera or ballet. The stories are familiar to the audience, which understands the various stage conventions that compensate for the lack of reality and reads the actors' face-paint to identify the characters they portray. Here the black and white represents a villain and the pheasant-feathers a graceful female warrior. In Singapore, most operas are staged on temporary street stages and are known by the Malay word for theatre,* wayang.

Following page
*Singapore: glittering city of the future, a place where skyscrapers sit side by side with colonial monuments of the past, where the abacus shares pride of place with the electronic calculator and the computer, where East meets West . . .*